Seventy-Eight Duets

for FLUTE and CLARINET

by HIMIE VOXMAN

PUBLISHED IN TWO VOLUMES

VOLUME I (Nos. 1 to 55)

Easy-Medium

VOLUME II (Nos. 56 to 78)

Advanced

RUBANK, INC.

HAL•LEONARD®
CORPORATION
7777 W. BLUEMOUND RD. P.O. BOX 13819 MILWAUKEE, WI 53213

Preface

Duet playing affords the student the most intimate form of ensemble experience. The problems of technique, tone quality, intonation, and ensemble balance are brought into the sharpest relief. Careful attention must be given to style as indicated by the printed page and as demanded by the intangibles of good taste.

The duets from the eighteenth century present many problems in the interpretation of ornaments. In the first volume the eighteenth century duets include those by various anonymous composers, and the Bachs, Boismortier, Dietter, Handel, the Mozarts, and others. In the advanced volume, in addition to the works of Bach and Mozart, those by Geminiani, Muffat, Quantz, Rameau,

and C. Stamitz are in this category. In general, trills written before the year 1800, and probably many written thereafter, should begin with the note *above* the principal note. The symbol ∿ is *not* a mordent in eighteenth century music, but a short trill.

For a more detailed treatment of the embellishments the performer is referred to the article on "Ornamentation" in the fifth edition of *Grove's Dictionary of Music and Musicians*, or the *Harvard Dictionary of Music*.

The author wishes to express his gratitude to the libraries of the *British Museum* (London), and the *Bibliothèque Nationale* (Paris), for the use of collections of wind music found in these institutions.

Himie Voxman

Menuet

LEOPOLD MOZART

Minuetto

LÖHLEIN

4

Moderato

GOEDICKE

Menuett

BACH

Allegretto

LÖHLEIN

C Flute

5

B♭ Clarinet

HOHMANN

Allegretto

C Flute

6

Bb Clarinet

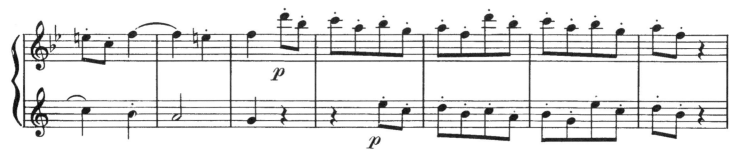

HOHMANN

Allegro

C Flute

7

Bb Clarinet

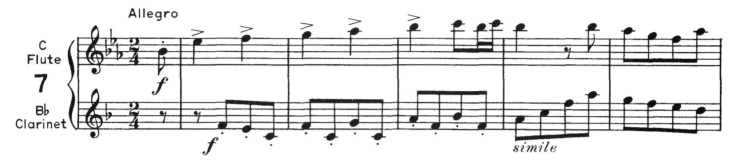

DIETTER

Tempo di Minuetto grazioso

C Flute

8

Bb Clarinet

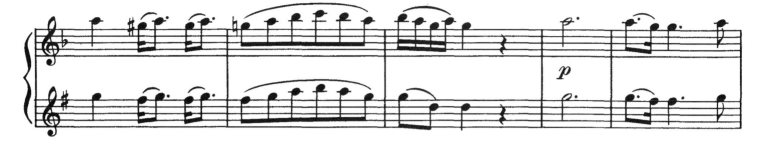

Menuett

FISCHER

C Flute
9
Bb Clarinet

WANHAL

Andante alla siciliano

C
Flute

10

Bb
Clarinet

Menuet

LEOPOLD MOZART

C. Ph. E. BACH

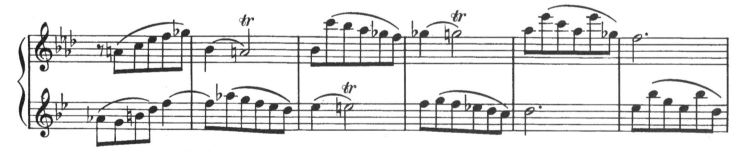

Menuetto

CAMPAGNOLI

KUMMER

14

C Flute

Bb Clarinet

Moderato

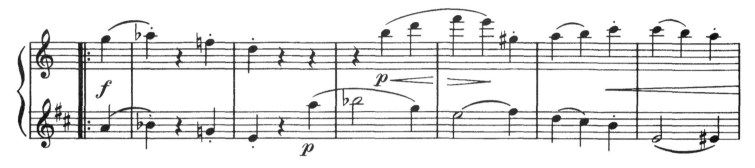

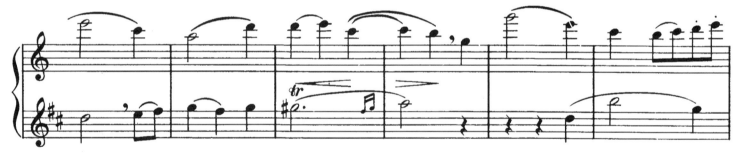

C. Ph. E. BACH

CAMPAGNOLI

BACH

Gigue
from Overture in F

BACH

Marsch

BACH

C Flute

19

Bb Clarinet

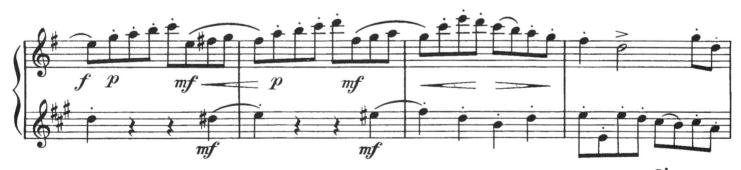

Bourrée

BACH

DURANTE

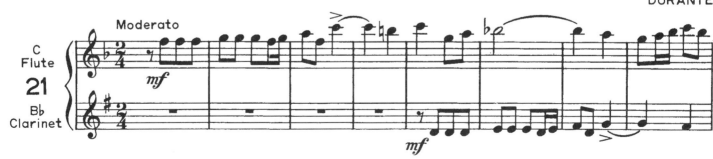

ALMENRAEDER

Allegro con moto

C
Flute

22

Bb
Clarinet

Romance

DIETTER

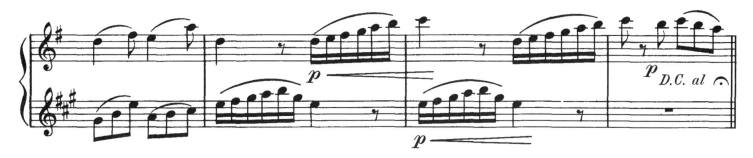

DIETTER

BÖHM

Minuetto

SALOMÉ

Gigue

BOISMORTIER

Canon

WORMSER

28

Allegro moderato

C Flute / Bb Clarinet

MOZART

29 C Flute / Bb Clarinet

Adagio

p

p

p

p

WANHAL

C Flute
30
Bb Clarinet

Allegretto

CODA

Sonatina

HANDEL

Allemande
(Suite XVI)

HANDEL

Canon

THOMÉ

Menuet

KRIEGER

FERLING

Poco adagio

C Flute

35

Bb Clarinet

Tambourin

CHEDEVILLE

Menuetto

MOZART

MAGNANI

MOZART

Allegro

C
Flute

39

Bb
Clarinet

Menuetto

MOZART

Bourée

Allegro molto

KRIEGER

C Flute

41

Bb Clarinet

Syncopation

CAMPAGNOLI

KRAKAMP

Allegretto moderato

Polonaise

GABRIELSKY

Polonaise da Capo

Syncopation

HOHMANN

Allegro

TELEMANN

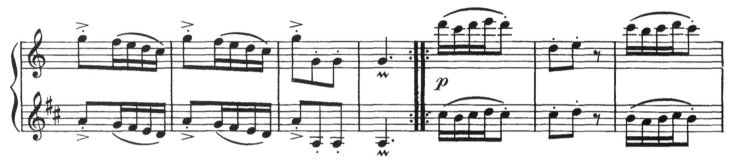

Rondeau

KRIEGER

SOUSSMANN

dim.

MAGNANI

Tempo di Minuetto

con slancio [impetuously]

p rall. assai

a tempo

f con slancio

p

a tempo

p

Divertissement No. 2

LEROY OSTRANSKY

Passepied

LACOME

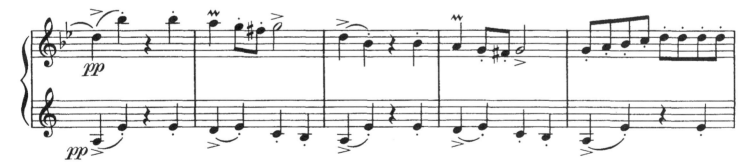

Rondo

FIALA

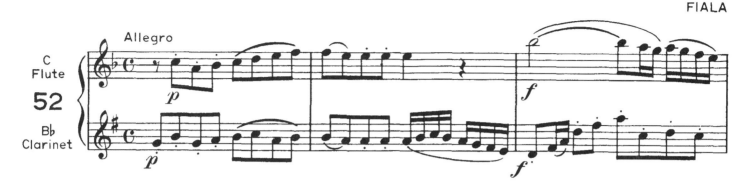

BLUMENTHAL

Allegro con spirito

C Flute

53

Bb Clarinet

KUMMER

Andante poco adagio

C
Flute

54

Bb
Clarinet

Sonatina
First Movement

LEROY OSTRANSKY

Allegro moderato

C Flute

55

Bb Clarinet

Meno mosso

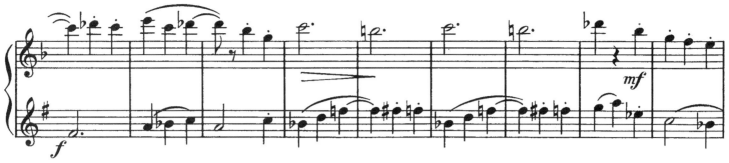

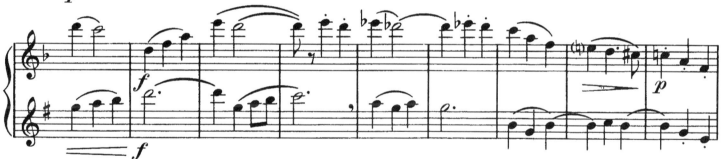

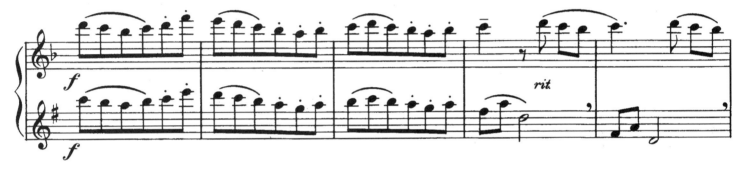